Great Works

Instructional Guides for Literature

How to Eat Fried Worms

A guide for the book by Thomas Rockwell
Great Works Author: Tracy Pearce

SHELL EDUCATION

Publishing Credits

Corinne Burton, M.A.Ed., *President*; Emily R. Smith, M.A.Ed., *Editorial Director*; Lee Aucoin, *Multimedia Designer*; Jill Mulhall, M.Ed., *Editor*; Stephanie Bernard, *Assistant Editor*; Don Tran, *Production Artist*; Amber Goff, *Editorial Assistant*

Image Credits

iStock (cover, page 12)

Standards

© 2007 Teachers of English to Speakers of Other Languages, Inc. (TESOL)
© 2007 Board of Regents of the University of Wisconsin System. World-Class Instructional Design and Assessment (WIDA)
© Copyright 2010. National Governors Association Center for Best Practices and Council of Chief State School Officers. All rights reserved.

Shell Education

5301 Oceanus Drive
Huntington Beach, CA 92649-1030
http://www.shelleducation.com
ISBN 978-1-4807-6994-6
© 2015 Shell Educational Publishing, Inc.

Table of Contents

How to Use This Literature Guide

Today's standards demand rigor and relevance in the reading of complex texts. The units in this series guide teachers in a rich and deep exploration of worthwhile works of literature for classroom study. The most rigorous instruction can also be interesting and engaging!

Many current strategies for effective literacy instruction have been incorporated into these instructional guides for literature. Throughout the units, text-dependent questions are used to determine comprehension of the book as well as student interpretation of the vocabulary words. The books chosen for the series are complex and are exemplars of carefully crafted works of literature. Close reading is used throughout the units to guide students toward revisiting the text and using textual evidence to respond to prompts orally and in writing. Students must analyze the story elements in multiple assignments for each section of the book. All of these strategies work together to rigorously guide students through their study of literature.

The next few pages describe how to use this guide for a purposeful and meaningful literature study. Each section of this guide is set up in the same way to make it easier for you to implement the instruction in your classroom.

Theme Thoughts

The great works of literature used throughout this series have important themes that have been relevant to people for many years. Many of the themes will be discussed during the various sections of this instructional guide. However, it would also benefit students to have independent time to think about the key themes of the book.

Before students begin reading, have them complete the *Pre-Reading Theme Thoughts* (page 13). This graphic organizer will allow students to think about the themes outside the context of the story. They'll have the opportunity to evaluate statements based on important themes and defend their opinions. Be sure to keep students' papers for comparison to the *Post-Reading Theme Thoughts* (page 61). This graphic organizer is similar to the pre-reading activity. However, this time, students will be answering the questions from the point of view of one of the characters in the book. They have to think about how the character would feel about each statement and defend their thoughts. To conclude the activity, have students compare what they thought about the themes before they read the book to what the characters discovered during the story.

Pre-Reading Picture Walks

For each section in this literature guide, there are suggestions for how to introduce the text to students. Teachers share information in a visual format and ask students to evaluate the content. Students must use the information presented in the illustrations to discuss what they are about to read and make predictions about the sections.

How to Use This Literature Guide (cont.)

Vocabulary

Each teacher reference vocabulary overview page has definitions and sentences about how key vocabulary words are used in the section. These words should be introduced and discussed with students. Students will use these words in different activities throughout the book.

On some of the vocabulary student pages, students are asked to answer text-related questions about vocabulary words from the sections. The following question stems will help you create your own vocabulary questions if you'd like to extend the discussion.

- How does this word describe _____'s character?
- How does this word connect to the problem in this story?
- How does this word help you understand the setting?
- Tell me how this word connects to the main idea of this story.
- What visual pictures does this word bring to your mind?
- Why do you think the author used this word?

At times, you may find that more work with the words will help students understand their meanings and importance. These quick vocabulary activities are a good way to further study the words.

- Students can play vocabulary concentration. Make one set of cards that has the words on them and another set with the definitions. Then, have students lay them out on the table and play concentration. The goal of the game is to match vocabulary words with their definitions. For early readers or English language learners, the two sets of cards could be the words and pictures of the words.
- Students can create word journal entries about the words. Students choose words they think are important and then describe why they think each word is important within the book. Early readers or English language learners could instead draw pictures about the words in a journal.
- Students can create puppets and use them to act out the vocabulary words from the stories. Students may also enjoy telling their own character-driven stories using vocabulary words from the original stories.

How to Use This Literature Guide (cont.)

Analyzing the Literature

After you have read each section with students, hold a small-group or whole-class discussion. Provided on the teacher reference page for each section are leveled questions. The questions are written at two levels of complexity to allow you to decide which questions best meet the needs of your students. The Level 1 questions are typically less abstract than the Level 2 questions. These questions are focused on the various story elements, such as character, setting, and plot. Be sure to add further questions as your students discuss what they've read. For each question, a few key points are provided for your reference as you discuss the book with students.

Reader Response

In today's classrooms, there are often great readers who are below average writers. So much time and energy is spent in classrooms getting students to read on grade level that little time is left to focus on writing skills. To help teachers include more writing in their daily literacy instruction, each section of this guide has a literature-based reader response prompt. Each of the three genres of writing is used in the reader responses within this guide: narrative, informative/explanatory, and opinion. Before students write, you may want to allow them time to draw pictures related to the topic. Book-themed writing paper is provided on page 69 if your students need more space to write.

Guided Close Reading

Within each section of this guide, it is suggested that you closely reread a portion of the text with your students. Page numbers are given, but since some versions of the books may have different page numbers, the sections to be reread are described by location as well. After rereading the section, there are a few text-dependent questions to be answered by students.

Working space has been provided to help students prepare for the group discussion. They should record their thoughts and ideas on the activity page and refer to it during your discussion. Rather than just taking notes, you may want to require students to write complete responses to the questions before discussing them with you.

Encourage students to read one question at a time and then go back to the text and discover the answer. Work with students to ensure that they use the text to determine their answers rather than making unsupported inferences. Suggested answers are provided in the answer key.

How to Use This Literature Guide (cont.)

Guided Close Reading (cont.)

The generic open-ended stems below can be used to write your own text-dependent questions if you would like to give students more practice.

- What words in the story support . . . ?
- What text helps you understand . . . ?
- Use the book to tell why _____ happens.
- Based on the events in the story, . . . ?
- Show me the part in the text that supports . . . .
- Use the text to tell why . . . .

Making Connections

The activities in this section help students make cross-curricular connections to mathematics, science, social studies, fine arts, or other curricular areas. These activities require higher-order thinking skills from students but also allow for creative thinking.

Language Learning

A special section has been set aside to connect the literature to language conventions. Through these activities, students will have opportunities to practice the conventions of standard English grammar, usage, capitalization, and punctuation.

Story Elements

It is important to spend time discussing what the common story elements are in literature. Understanding the characters, setting, plot, and theme can increase students' comprehension and appreciation of the story. If teachers begin discussing these elements in early childhood, students will more likely internalize the concepts and look for the elements in their independent reading. Another very important reason for focusing on the story elements is that students will be better writers if they think about how the stories they read are constructed.

In the story elements activities, students are asked to create work related to the characters, setting, or plot. Consider having students complete only one of these activities. If you give students a choice on this assignment, each student can decide to complete the activity that most appeals to him or her. Different intelligences are used so that the activities are diverse and interesting to all students.

How to Use This Literature Guide (cont.)

Culminating Activity

At the end of this instructional guide is a creative culminating activity that allows students the opportunity to share what they've learned from reading the book. This activity is open ended so that students can push themselves to create their own great works within your language arts classroom.

Comprehension Assessment

The questions in this section require students to think about the book they've read as well as the words that were used in the book. Some questions are tied to quotations from the book to engage students and require them to think about the text as they answer the questions.

Response to Literature

Finally, students are asked to respond to the literature by drawing pictures and writing about the characters and stories. A suggested rubric is provided for teacher reference.

Correlation to the Standards

Shell Education is committed to producing educational materials that are research and standards based. As part of this effort, we have correlated all of our products to the academic standards of all 50 states, the District of Columbia, the Department of Defense Dependents Schools, and all Canadian provinces.

Purpose and Intent of Standards

Standards are designed to focus instruction and guide adoption of curricula. Standards are statements that describe the criteria necessary for students to meet specific academic goals. They define the knowledge, skills, and content students should acquire at each level. Standards are also used to develop standardized tests to evaluate students' academic progress. Teachers are required to demonstrate how their lessons meet standards. Standards are used in the development of all of our products, so educators can be assured they meet high academic standards.

How to Find Standards Correlations

To print a customized correlation report of this product for your state, visit our website at http://www.shelleducation.com and follow the online directions. If you require assistance in printing correlation reports, please contact our Customer Service Department at 1-877-777-3450.

Correlation to the Standards (cont.)

Standards Correlation Chart

The lessons in this book were written to support today's college and career readiness standards. The following chart indicates which lessons address the standards.

College and Career Readiness Standard	Section
Read closely to determine what the text says explicitly and to make logical inferences from it; cite specific textual evidence when writing or speaking to support conclusions drawn from the text. (R.1)	Guided Close Reading Sections 1–5; Vocabulary Activity Sections 1–5; Story Elements Sections 4–5; Post-Reading Response to Literature
Determine central ideas or themes of a text and analyze their development; summarize the key supporting details and ideas. (R.2)	Analyzing the Literature Sections 1–5; Guided Close Reading Sections 1–5; Theme Thoughts; Culminating Activity
Analyze how and why individuals, events, or ideas develop and interact over the course of a text. (R.3)	Analyzing the Literature Sections 1–5; Story Elements Sections 2–3, 5; Post-Reading Theme Thoughts; Culminating Activity; Post-Reading Response to Literature
Interpret words and phrases as they are used in a text, including determining technical, connotative, and figurative meanings, and analyze how specific word choices shape meaning or tone. (R.4)	Guided Close Reading Sections 1–5; Vocabulary Activity Sections 1–5; Language Learning Sections 3–4; Story Elements Section 2
Analyze the structure of texts, including how specific sentences, paragraphs, and larger portions of the text (e.g., a section, chapter, scene, or stanza) relate to each other and the whole. (R.5)	Guided Close Reading Sections 1–5
Read and comprehend complex literary and informational texts independently and proficiently. (R.10)	Guided Close Reading Sections 1–5; Making Connections Section 2; Story Elements Sections 3–4;
Write arguments to support claims in an analysis of substantive topics or texts using valid reasoning and relevant and sufficient evidence. (W.1)	Reader Response Sections 3–4; Guided Close Reading Sections 1–5; Story Elements Sections 1–5; Post-Reading Theme Thoughts; Culminating Activity; Post-Reading Response to Literature
Write informative/explanatory texts to examine and convey complex ideas and information clearly and accurately through the effective selection, organization, and analysis of content. (W.2)	Reader Response Section 5; Making Connections Section 4
Write narratives to develop real or imagined experiences or events using effective technique, well-chosen details and well-structured event sequences. (W.3)	Reader Response Sections 1–2; Story Elements Sections 1–2
Produce clear and coherent writing in which the development, organization, and style are appropriate to task, purpose, and audience. (W.4)	Guided Close Reading Sections 1–5; Reader Response Sections 1–5; Story Elements Sections 2–3; Post-Reading Theme Thoughts; Culminating Activity; Post-Reading Response to Literature

College and Career Readiness Standard	Section
Demonstrate command of the conventions of standard English grammar and usage when writing or speaking. (L.1)	Guided Close Reading Sections 1–5; Vocabulary Activity Sections 1–5; Making Connections Section 4; Language Learning Sections 1, 4; Story Elements Sections 1–5; Post-Reading Theme Thoughts; Culminating Activity; Post-Reading Response to Literature
Demonstrate command of the conventions of standard English capitalization, punctuation, and spelling when writing. (L.2)	Guided Close Reading Sections 1–5; Vocabulary Activity Sections 1–5; Story Elements Sections 1–5; Making Connections Section 4; Language Learning Section 5; Post-Reading Theme Thoughts; Culminating Activity; Post-Reading Response to Literature
Apply knowledge of language to understand how language functions in different contexts, to make effective choices for meaning or style, and to comprehend more fully when reading or listening. (L.3)	Analyzing the Literature Sections 1–5; Guided Close Reading Sections 1–5; Language Learning Sections 2–3; Story Elements Section 3
Determine or clarify the meaning of unknown and multiple-meaning words and phrases by using context clues, analyzing meaningful word parts, and consulting general and specialized reference materials, as appropriate. (L.4)	Vocabulary Sections 1–5; Language Learning Section 3
Demonstrate understanding of figurative language, word relationships, and nuances in word meanings. (L.5)	Language Learning Section 4
Acquire and use accurately a range of general academic and domain-specific words and phrases sufficient for reading, writing, speaking, and listening at the college and career readiness level; demonstrate independence in gathering vocabulary knowledge when encountering an unknown term important to comprehension or expression. (L.6)	Vocabulary Sections 1–5; Analyzing the Literature Sections 1–5; Guided Close Reading Sections 1–5; Making Connections Sections 1, 5; Post-Reading Theme Thoughts; Culminating Activity; Post-Reading Response to Literature

TESOL and WIDA Standards

The lessons in this book promote English language development for English language learners. The following TESOL and WIDA English Language Development Standards are addressed through the activities in this book:

- **Standard 1:** English language learners communicate for social and instructional purposes within the school setting.

- **Standard 2:** English language learners communicate information, ideas and concepts necessary for academic success in the content area of language arts.

About the Author—Thomas Rockwell

Thomas Rockwell was born in March 1933 in New Rochelle, New York. He is the son of artist Norman Rockwell, who is famous for his iconic paintings of American life done for *The Saturday Evening Post*. At age five, Rockwell moved to rural Vermont. During his boyhood years he worked on a local farm gathering hay. Rockwell knew early on that he wanted to be a writer. He attended Princeton University for a short time, and went on to graduate from Bard College in 1956.

After college, Rockwell worked for a gardening magazine in New York. He left that job to help his father write his autobiography. Rockwell's first children's book, *Rackety-Bang, and Other Verses*, received such terrible reviews that his publisher declined his next book of verse. Rockwell switched to novels, and he published several more children's books before writing the one for which he is best known, *How to Eat Fried Worms*. The inspiration for the novel came out of a feeling of unhappiness following an editorial meeting about another book that did not go well. Rockwell felt upset enough to eat worms. Immediately he decided he wanted to write a book about a young boy who eats fried worms. *How to Eat Fried Worms* was rejected by 23 publishers before it was published by Yearling in 1973.

How to Eat Fried Worms gained Rockwell national attention. The book won ten awards, including the Mark Twain Award, the Golden Archer Award, the Sequoiah Award, and The Nene Award. The book also garnered controversy over the years, as disapproval of its depictions of worm eating and gambling ensured its repeated inclusion on the list of the 100 most banned and challenged books in school libraries.

Rockwell wrote two sequels to his most successful novel, called *How to Fight a Girl* and *How to Get Fabulously Rich*. He also wrote several other novels, and he worked as a writer for television and advertising. *How to Eat Fried Worms* was made into an animated 30-minute film for CBS in 1985 and into a full-length motion picture in 2006. Rockwell currently resides in New York.

Possible Texts for Text Comparisons

Thomas Rockwell wrote the books *How to Fight a Girl* and *How to Get Fabulously Rich* as sequels to *How to Eat Fried Worms*. These books center on the continuing adventures of the main character, Billy Forrester.

Book Summary of *How to Eat Fried Worms*

A group of young friends finds themselves having a discussion about what foods they would be willing to try rather than being sent to their rooms for refusing to eat supper. Billy boasts that he would eat anything, including mud and worms. Alan doesn't believe his friend, and he bets Billy 50 dollars that he can't eat 15 worms in 15 days. Billy has doubts about his ability to eat the worms, but he is tempted by the money, which he could use to buy a mini-bike. After some goading by Alan and their other friends, Tom and Joe, Billy agrees to the bet.

The four boys all agree that Billy can eat the worms with any condiment he chooses and can cook them any way he likes. At first, Billy struggles to down the worms. But within a few days it becomes easier for him, and it seems inevitable that he will win the bet. Alan and Joe become increasingly desperate to stop Billy from eating the 15 worms. They carry out a variety of tricks and sabotages designed to keep Billy from being successful. The tension between the four once-close friends grows and eventually leads them to decidedly unfriendly behaviors, including threats, lies, name-calling, and a physical fight.

In the end, Billy succeeds in his quest to win the bet and Alan has no choice but to pay up. The boys' friendship is damaged but shows signs of surviving.

Cross-Curricular Connection

This book can be used in a science unit on worms or in a social science unit on friendship.

Possible Texts for Text Sets

- Blume, Judy. *Tales of a Fourth Grade Nothing*. Penguin Group, 2007.
- Catling, Patrick Skene. *The Chocolate Touch*. HarperCollins Publishers, 2006.
- Cleary, Beverly. *Ramona the Brave*. HarperCollins Publishers, 1995.
- Clements, Andrew. *Frindle*. Atheneum Books for Young Readers, 1998.
- DeClements, Barthe. *Nothing's Fair in Fifth Grade*. Penguin Group, 2008.
- Smith, Robert Kimmel. *Chocolate Fever*. Penguin Group, 2006.

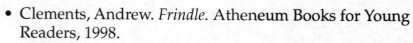

Name _____ Date _____

Pre-Reading Theme Thoughts

Directions: Draw a picture of a happy face or a sad face. Your face should show how you feel about each statement. Then, use words to say what you think about each statement.

Statement	How Do You Feel? 🙂 🙁	Explain Your Answer
Bets are fun to make but hard to keep.		
When kids are worried, they should talk to their parents.		
Friends disagree sometimes.		
Cheating is not fair.		

Vocabulary Overview

Key words and phrases from this section are provided below with definitions and sentences about how the words are used in the story. Introduce and discuss these important vocabulary words with students. If you think these words or other words in the story warrant more time devoted to them, there are suggestions in the introduction for other vocabulary activities (page 5).

Word	Definition	Sentence about Text
fricasseed (ch. 1)	meat that is cut into small pieces, stewed in liquid, and served in a thick sauce	Billy can eat the worms boiled, stewed, fried, or **fricasseed**.
witnesses (ch. 1)	persons who are present at an event and see it take place	There must be **witnesses** present when Billy eats worms.
manure (ch. 2)	solid waste from farm animals that is used to make soil better for growing plants	Tom thinks it is unfair to dig up a worm from the **manure** pile.
orange crate (ch. 3)	a slatted wooden box for packing, shipping, or storing oranges	Billy blocks the door with an **orange crate** to keep the dogs inside.
piccalilli (ch. 3)	a pickled relish made of various chopped vegetables and hot spices	Billy sets up bottles and jars of various condiments, including **piccalilli**.
sprawled (ch. 4)	to be stretched or spread out in an unnatural or unattractive fashion	The huge night crawler **sprawls** limply on the platter.
fink (ch. 4)	someone who does not do what they said they were going to do	When Billy hesitates about eating the night crawler, Alan calls him a **fink**.
menacingly (ch. 4)	in a threatening manner	Tom gets nervous when Billy tiptoes **menacingly** around him.
daub (ch. 6)	a smear that is messily applied to something	The last bite of worm sits under a **daub** of ketchup and mustard.
chaff (ch. 6)	the discarded husks and debris that come off of seed when it is threshed	Billy lies on his back in the **chaff** that litters the horse barn.

Vocabulary Activity

Directions: Write five sentences about the story. Use at least one vocabulary word from the box below in each sentence.

Words from the Story

fricasseed	witnesses	manure	orange crate	piccalilli
sprawled	fink	menacingly	daub	chaff

_____

_____

_____

_____

_____

_____

_____

Directions: Answer this question.

1. Why do the boys want **witnesses** when Billy eats the worms?

_____

_____

Analyzing the Literature

Provided here are discussion questions you can use in small groups, with the whole class, or for written assignments. Each question is written at two levels so that you can choose the right question for each group of students. For each question, a few key points are provided for your reference as you discuss the book with students.

Story Element	Level 1	Level 2	Key Discussion Points
Plot	What bet do the boys make?	What specific rules do the boys make about their bet?	Alan bets Billy 50 dollars that Billy will not be able to eat 15 worms in 15 days. Billy has to eat one worm a day. He can eat the worms any way he wants: boiled, stewed, fried, or fricasseed. He can also use any condiments. Alan and Joe will provide the worms, which they agree cannot be big green ones from the tomato plants. There must be witnesses present when Billy eats the worms.
Character	What do you know about Billy's looks and his personality?	What traits of Billy's suggest that he might win the bet?	Billy is chunky, snub-nosed, and freckled. He likes all kinds of food, even food that other kids don't. Billy takes on many dares that other kids offer him. He is stubborn, and takes pride in following through when he says he will do something. Billy also has a sense of humor, scaring Alan and Joe after he finishes eating the first worm.
Setting	What is the setting of chapter 2?	Describe the setting of chapter 2. Be sure to include sensory details.	Tom, Alan, and Joe are wandering behind the barns at Billy's house. They are arguing about where to dig up the first worm. They can't decide if the worm can come from a stinky manure pile. They walk across the field dragging shovels. They stop and talk under a tree in the apple orchard.
Plot	Why does Billy get mad right before he eats the first worm?	Why does Billy agree to eat the night crawler even though he thinks it is unfair?	Billy gets mad when he sees the big night crawler he has to eat. He says a night crawler is not a worm. Billy thinks it is not fair. Alan reminds Billy that they agreed at the start that he and Joe could choose the worms. Tom warns Billy that everyone will think he is chicken if he doesn't eat the worm. Billy reluctantly eats it, piece by piece.

Reader Response

Think

Think about a time when you did not want to eat your dinner. Did you dislike the taste of the meal or what it looked like? Think about why you did not want to eat it.

Narrative Writing Prompt

Think about a food that you do not like to eat. Explain why you do not like it and do not want to eat it.

_____

_____

_____

_____

_____

_____

_____

_____

_____

Guided Close Reading

Closely reread the section that starts at the beginning of chapter 2 and ends with, "You know what I mean."

Directions: Think about these questions. In the space below, write ideas as you think about the answers. Be ready to share your answers.

❶ Use details from the text to describe what the boys are arguing about.

❷ What words does Joe use in the passage to explain that there is nothing wrong with manure?

❸ Look back at the book. What does Tom ask Alan and Joe to make them consider whether they are being fair?

Making Connections–
Yummy Foods and Yucky Foods

Directions: Tom does not want to eat his dinner. It is salmon casserole. On the plate below, draw yummy foods that you enjoy eating and yucky foods that you do not like to eat.

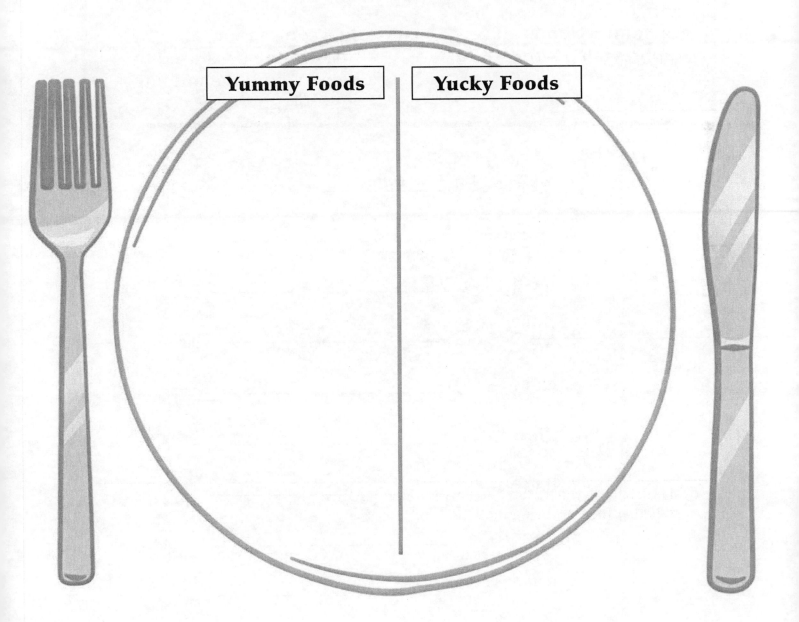

Yummy Foods   **Yucky Foods**

Name _____ Date _____

Language Learning–Spelling

Directions: The first part of *How to Eat Fried Worms* uses many contractions. Read the list of contractions from the story below. Next to each contraction, write the two words that make up the contraction.

Language Hints!

- A **contraction** is an abbreviated word.

- In a contraction, an apostrophe (') is used to show where the missing letter(s) go.

1. what's _____*what*_____ ___*is*___

2. wouldn't _____ _____

3. hasn't _____ _____

4. I'll _____ _____

5. can't _____ _____

6. didn't _____ _____

7. hadn't _____ _____

8. they'll _____ _____

9. it'll _____ _____

10. he's _____ _____

Story Elements-Setting

Directions: Draw a picture of the setting when Billy eats the first worm. Make sure to include details of where he sits, what he holds, and what he wears. Then, write at least two sentences describing your picture.

_____

_____

_____

_____

Name _____ Date _____

Story Elements-Plot

Directions: Make a prediction. Do you think Billy will be able to successfully eat the 15 worms in 15 days and win the bet? Make sure to include reasons to support your answer.

_____

_____

_____

_____

_____

_____

_____

_____

_____

_____

_____

Vocabulary Overview

Key words and phrases from this section are provided below with definitions and sentences about how the words are used in the story. Introduce and discuss these important vocabulary words with students. If you think these words or other words in the story warrant more time devoted to them, there are suggestions in the introduction for other vocabulary activities (page 5).

Word	Definition	Sentence about Text
gaggles (ch. 7)	flocks or groups	Poor Billy can't help but think of **gaggles** of worms.
gores (ch. 7)	pierces or stabs with something pointed	Billy imagines a worm squirming as the fishhook **gores** into him.
steadily (ch. 10)	regularly and continually	Billy eats **steadily,** making his way through the fourth worm.
hobble (ch. 10)	to walk in an awkward way because of injury or weakness	Alan is laughing so hard, he has to **hobble** off into one of the horse stalls to recover.
lolling (ch. 10)	hanging loosely	Joe describes his mother, collapsed with her tongue **lolling** out of her mouth.
apoplectically (ch. 10)	extremely angrily; furiously	Insulted by the boys' comments about his mother, Joe yells **apoplectically.**
sullenly (ch. 10)	grumpily; showing irritation	Still upset, Joe glances **sullenly** back at Billy.
hayloft (ch. 11)	the upper part of a barn or stable where hay is stored	Alan and Joe look down on Billy from their perch in the **hayloft.**
glimpse (ch. 11)	a very quick, passing look at something	Billy spins around just in time to catch a **glimpse** of Tom running out the door.
clambering (ch. 11)	climbing in an awkward way	Anxious to get away from Billy, Tom **clambers** over the meadow wall.

Name _____ Date _____

Vocabulary Activity

Directions: Draw lines to complete the sentences.

Beginning of Sentences

Billy eats **steadily**,

I can't help thinking of

Alan and Joe watch from above,

Billy spins around just in time to catch

Joe looks at Billy **sullenly**

Endings of Sentences

a worm squirming as the fishhook **gores** into him.

because he is upset about something that Billy said.

grimacing, rubbing his nose, spreading on horseradish.

a **glimpse** of Tom pelting out the door.

lying on their stomachs in the **hayloft**.

Directions: Answer this question.

1. Why is Billy constantly thinking of **gaggles** of worms?

_____

_____

Analyzing the Literature

Provided here are discussion questions you can use in small groups, with the whole class, or for written assignments. Each question is written at two levels so that you can choose the right question for each group of students. For each question, a few key points are provided for your reference as you discuss the book with students.

Story Element	Level 1	Level 2	Key Discussion Points
Plot	What strategy does Billy use to make it easier to eat the third worm?	How does Tom help Billy eat the third worm? What motivation does Tom have to help Billy win?	The first two worms are simply boiled. Tom fries the third worm in cornmeal. He thinks that if he makes the worm seem like fish, with parsley and some slices of lemon around it, it will be easier for Billy to eat. Tom also sings some funny fish songs and tells Billy to keep thinking fish, fish, fish, fish. Tom wants Billy to win because if Billy wins, he will buy a mini-bike and let Tom use it.
Character	What trick do Alan and Joe play on Billy in chapter 10?	Describe the trick that Alan and Joe play on Billy in chapter 10. What does this development tell us about Alan and Joe?	With Alan's help, Joe makes up a story to scare Billy so he will stop eating the worms and hence lose the bet. Joe pretends that his mother and father are crazy with fear that Joe may have eaten a worm. He makes his story dramatic and indicates that the potential consequences of eating a worm are horrifying. Billy is very scared, but Tom doesn't believe Joe and Alan. He recognizes that the boys can't keep straight faces, and that they are just making up the story. Here, we learn that Alan and Joe are unscrupulous and willing to cheat and lie to win the bet.
Setting	In chapter 13, Alan calls Joe on the phone. What time do you think it is when he makes this call?	Alan gets out of bed and calls Joe in chapter 13. What is the significance of the fact that this call is made late at night?	It is nighttime when Alan makes the call, probably very late. Alan has been in bed, unable to sleep. He has to convince Mrs. O'Hara, Joe's mother, to wake Joe so he can speak to him. The timing of this call tells us that Alan is in a panic about losing the bet and having to hand over 50 dollars. He would never make a phone call so late at night if he were not desperate.

Name _____ Date _____

Reader Response

Think

Billy makes a bet to eat 15 worms. Have you ever made a bet with someone? Has someone ever dared you to do something?

Narrative Writing Prompt

Write about a bet you have made. If you have not made a bet before, write about a bet you would like to make.

_____

_____

_____

_____

_____

_____

_____

_____

_____

Guided Close Reading

Closely reread chapter 12, "The Fifth Worm."

Directions: Think about these questions. In the space below, write ideas as you think about the answers. Be ready to share your answers.

❶ What evidence supports the idea that Alan and Joe are trying to hurry Billy, hoping to make him quit?

❷ What text shows that Alan and Joe think Billy is going to lose the bet?

❸ Describe, specifically, what Billy does after he eats the fifth worm.

Making Connections-All About Earthworms

Directions: Below are 12 interesting details about earthworms. Cut apart the cards. Glue each one on page 29 under the main idea that it matches.

Earthworms have no arms, legs, lungs, or eyes.	Earthworms live in soil, trees, and under rocks.	In the Philippines there are blue earthworms.
Earthworms live where there is food, moisture, oxygen, and a good temperature.	Earthworms breathe through their skin. They surface after heavy rains so they do not drown.	The night crawler gets its name because it typically surfaces after dark.
Even though earthworms have no eyes, they can sense light.	There are thousands of different kinds of earthworms.	South African earthworms can grow to be 22 feet (6.71 meters) long.
Earthworms have five hearts.	Each earthworm is both male and female.	Earthworms can burrow up to six feet (1.83 meters) deep.

Making Connections-All About Earthworms (cont.)

Directions: Cut apart the supporting details about earthworms found on page 28 and glue each one under the main idea that it matches.

The Body of an Earthworm	Where Earthworms Live	Different Kinds of Earthworms

Name _____ Date _____

Language Learning–Adjectives

Directions: Think of adjectives to describe the worms that Billy has to eat. Draw a picture of a worm like one that Billy has to eat. Then, write many creative adjectives around the worm.

Language Hints!

- An adjective is a word that describes a noun.

Story Elements-Character

Directions: Tom makes up a song to make it easier for Billy to eat the third worm. Make up a song or poem that would make it easier for you to do something you don't like to do. Try to make your song or poem rhyme.

Name _____ Date _____

Story Elements-Plot

Directions: Describe in words or pictures three main events from this section. Make sure they are in chronological order.

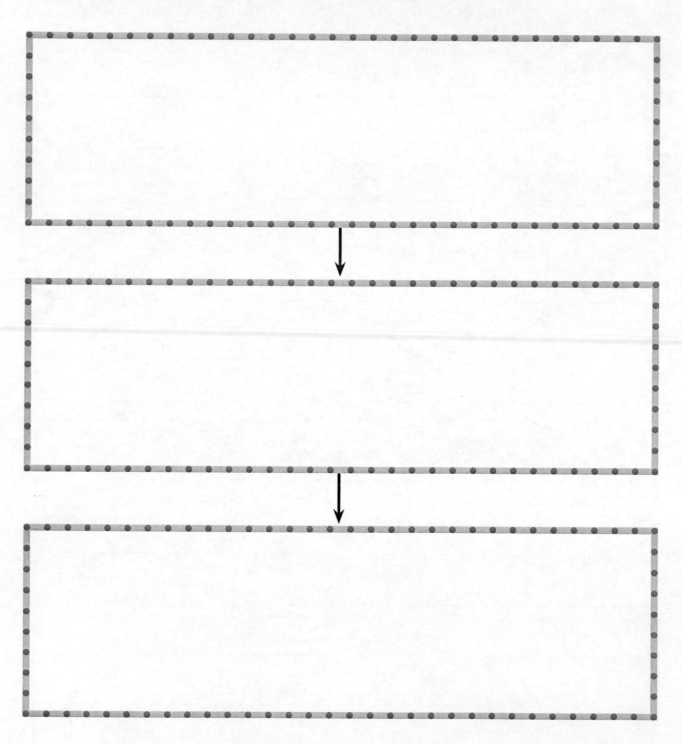

Vocabulary Overview

Key words and phrases from this section are provided below with definitions and sentences about how the words are used in the story. Introduce and discuss these important vocabulary words with students. If you think these words or other words in the story warrant more time devoted to them, there are suggestions in the introduction for other vocabulary activities (page 5).

Word	Definition	Sentence about Text
butcher shop (ch. 14)	a shop where meats and poultry are sold	Billy dreams that he is ordering worms in a busy **butcher shop**.
mammoth (ch. 14)	huge	In his dream, Billy cuts into one of the **mammoth** black worms.
shutter (ch. 14)	one of a pair of covers for a window that opens and closes like a door	When he wakes in the middle of the night, Billy hears a **shutter** bang in the wind.
antidote (ch. 14)	a medicine that is taken to stop the harmful effects of a specific poison	Bent over in pain, Billy hopes there is an **antidote** for eating worms.
triumphantly (ch. 16)	celebrating victory or success	Billy gulps the worm **triumphantly**, with an untroubled look on his face.
lurked (ch. 16)	waited in a hidden place	Tom **lurks** sheepishly in the bushes outside the barn.
glumly (ch. 17)	sadly or moodily	Alan and Joe **glumly** watch Billy eat the seventh worm.
tentatively (ch. 17)	hesitantly	Nervous Tom waves **tentatively** at Billy through the window.
gnawed (ch. 18)	bit or chewed something repeatedly	Alan **gnaws** at his thumbnail as he thinks about the 50 dollars he might lose.
disdainfully (ch. 18)	showing scorn or disapproval	Billy greets Tom **disdainfully** and walks on.

Name _____ Date _____

Vocabulary Activity

Directions: Complete each sentence below with one of the vocabulary words from the story.

Words from the Story

butcher shop	mammoth	shutter	antidote	triumphantly
lurks	glumly	tentatively	gnaws	disdainfully

1. Alan is so worried about the bet, he _____ at his fingernails.

2. Billy dreams he must eat a _____ worm.

3. Tom is unsure of how Billy feels, so he waves _____ at Billy.

4. Outside, the wind blows and Billy hears a _____ banging.

Directions: Answer this question.

5. Why does Billy think he needs an **antidote**?

_____

_____

_____

Analyzing the Literature

Provided here are discussion questions you can use in small groups, with the whole class, or for written assignments. Each question is written at two levels so that you can choose the right question for each group of students. For each question, a few key points are provided for your reference as you discuss the book with students.

Story Element	Level 1	Level 2	Key Discussion Points
Plot	Why does Billy go to his parents' bedroom in the middle of the night?	Describe what happens when Billy goes to his parents' bedroom. How do his parents react to what he says?	Billy has a nightmare about eating worms, and wakes to find his stomach rumbling and gurgling. He goes to his parents and tells them that he has been eating worms. His mother is very upset and wants to call the doctor. His father takes the news calmly, saying Billy will be fine. They argue; eventually Billy's father gives in and calls Poison Control.
Character	How does Alan feel as Billy begins to have no trouble eating the worms?	What details in the book tell you that Alan is feeling desperate that he might lose the bet?	Alan is extremely worried that Billy doesn't seem to be cracking. He regrets making the bet. His mind races, he looks glum, he bites his fingernails, he worries about his father's reaction, and he can't get the 50 dollars out of his head. Eventually, Alan tries to trick Billy by gluing two worms together.
Setting	Describe the setting when Billy wakes up after his nightmare.	When Billy wakes up after his nightmare, how does the setting help add to his rising panic?	When Billy wakes up, it is the middle of the night. The moon shines into the room, leaves blow in the wind outside, and a shutter bangs. Billy is already worried about eating the worms and is traumatized by his nightmare. The late hour and spooky mood make his concerns seem scarier and more real.
Plot	After Alan glues the two worms together, is the bet still on?	Why do the boys decide that the bet is still on, even after Alan tries to cheat in chapter 19?	After an argument, the boys decide that, despite Alan's machinations, the bet will continue. Joe successfully contends that the bet is still valid since Billy didn't actually eat two worms. Since the trick didn't work, he says, it doesn't count as actually cheating. Only if Billy had fallen for the trick would it have nullified the bet.

Reader Response

Think

Alan and Joe glue two worms together to make an enormous worm. Think about whether you think it is fair for Alan and Joe to do this.

Opinion Writing Prompt

Tell your opinion about whether it is fair for the boys to glue two worms together. Make sure to give the reasons why you think it is fair or unfair.

_____

_____

_____

_____

_____

_____

_____

_____

Guided Close Reading

Closely reread chapter 18, "The Eighth Worm."

Directions: Think about these questions. In the space below, write ideas as you think about the answers. Be ready to share your answers.

---

❶ Look back at the book to remember how Billy eats the eighth worm. What does he put on the worm?

---

❷ What words or actions show that Alan is worried about losing the bet?

---

❸ How does Billy react when Alan tries to scare him? What does he say to Alan?

Name _____ Date _____

Making Connections–Wormy Math

Directions: Read the wormy word problems below. Solve each math problem and write the answer.

1. If Billy had to eat 30 worms in 5 days, how many worms does he need to eat each day?

2. If Billy ate 3 worms a day for 15 days, how many worms would he eat altogether?

3. If Billy had to eat 45 worms in 9 days, how many worms does he need to eat each day?

Directions: Write your own wormy word problem below. Then, give your paper to a friend and have him or her solve the problem.

_____

_____

Language Learning-Meanings of Words

Directions: Look at the words below. Use a dictionary to find the meanings of the words as they are used in the story. Write the meaning of each word next to it in the chart.

Vocabulary Word	Definition from the Story
jostled (chapter 14)	
discernible (chapter 15)	
serene (chapter 16)	
glowered (chapter 16)	
sheepishly (chapter 16)	

Name _____ Date _____

Story Elements-Character

Directions: Which character in *How to Eat Fried Worms* do you like best? Give at least three reasons for your answer.

_____

_____

_____

_____

_____

_____

_____

_____

_____

_____

_____

_____

Name _____ Date _____

Story Elements-Plot

Directions: In chapter 14, Billy has a nightmare. Draw a picture of him lying in his bed having his bad dream. Write the main events of the nightmare in chronological order in the bubbles above him.

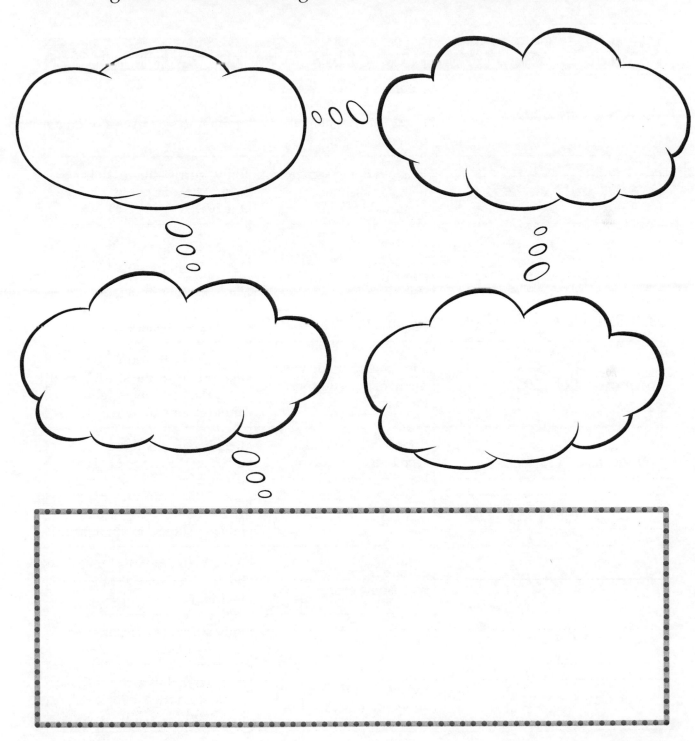

Vocabulary Overview

Key words and phrases from this section are provided below with definitions and sentences about how the words are used in the story. Introduce and discuss these important vocabulary words with students. If you think these words or other words in the story warrant more time devoted to them, there are suggestions in the introduction for other vocabulary activities (page 5).

Word	Definition	Sentence about Text
referee (ch. 20)	a person who makes sure that players act according to the rules of a game or sport	Joe and Alan ask Billy's mother to step in as a **referee**.
weasel out (ch. 20)	to avoid doing something by being dishonest or sneaky	Billy worries that Alan is trying to **weasel out** of the bet.
distaste (ch. 22)	a strong feeling of not liking someone or something	Emily eyes the Whizbang Worm Delight with **distaste**.
slumped (ch. 23)	sat limply, bent over	A worried Alan sits **slumped** on the porch steps.
murmur (ch. 28)	a low sound made when many people are speaking far away	A confused **murmur** rises up and down the street after the boys' late-night announcement.
furtively (ch. 28)	done in a quiet and secretive way to avoid being noticed	Joe peers **furtively** out through the fringe of his bedspread.
tramped (ch. 28)	walked wearily	Alan and Joe **tramp** from house to house to apologize.
incident (ch. 28)	a troubling or worrisome event	Alan's father warns him that he does not want another **incident**.
clenched (ch. 29)	held tightly closed	Billy sneers at Alan through **clenched** teeth.
wrenched away (ch. 29)	twisted and pulled with a sudden violent motion	Billy **wrenches away** when Tom tries to look at his wound.

Vocabulary Activity

Directions: Complete each sentence by choosing the correct vocabulary word and writing it on the line.

1. Alan is very worried and is _____ on
   (tramped; clumped)

   the porch steps gazing down at his sneakers.

2. The boys heard a confused _____
   (murmur; incident)

   from all of the neighbors looking out of their houses.

3. Billy is so angry at Alan he speaks to him through

   _____ teeth.
   (clenched; furtively)

4. Billy accuses Alan of wanting to _____
   (weasel out; wrench away)

   of the bet.

Directions: Answer this question.

5. Why does Joe say that Billy's mother will make a good **referee**?

   _____

   _____

   _____

Analyzing the Literature

Provided here are discussion questions you can use in small groups, with the whole class, or for written assignments. Each question is written at two levels so that you can choose the right question for each group of students. For each question, a few key points are provided for your reference as you discuss the book with students.

Story Element	Level 1	Level 2	Key Discussion Points
Plot	Why do Alan and Joe come to Billy's house in chapter 20?	Do you think Alan and Joe have a hidden motivation when they come talk to Billy's mother?	Alan and Joe come to see Mrs. Forrester because they are going away on a fishing trip. They want Billy's mother to be a referee and to make sure Billy eats his worms while they are out of town. The boys may also hope that if they "tattle" on Billy, his mother will be upset and will force Billy to stop eating worms.
Plot	How does Mrs. Forrester prepare the eleventh worm?	Billy's mother creates the Whizbang Worm Delight for the eleventh worm. How is her creation helpful to Billy?	Mrs. Forrester creates the Whizbang Worm Delight for the eleventh worm. It is an ice-cream cake with fruit syrups, whipped cream, jellybeans, and almond slivers, served on a silver dish. Billy's mother makes eating the worm almost enjoyable. She also shows her support for Billy, and she alleviates any residual fears he might have about his health.
Setting	What new setting is introduced in chapter 20 and revisited several times in the following chapters?	In this section, Billy's kitchen becomes a recurring setting. How does this seem to affect the way Billy handles the eating of the worms?	Most of the book so far has taken place in the barn. At this point, Billy begins eating the worms at home, in his kitchen. Billy and his mother put the next few worms into dishes. This seems to make it much easier for Billy to eat them. Being in a kitchen might help him think of the worms as food.
Character	What happens among the four friends in chapter 29?	Why do you think these four once-close friends end up in a physical fight in chapter 29?	The boys start calling each other names and making threats. They then have an ugly fistfight. It's obvious that the pressure of the bet has created problems in their friendship. Alan is desperate about the 50 dollars, Billy is angry about Alan's various tricks, and Joe and Tom feel loyal to their respective sides.

Reader Response

Think

Alan and Joe try to distract Billy from eating the thirteenth worm by bringing him to a Mets game, filling him up on junk food, and bringing him home late. Is this cheating or just good strategy?

Opinion Writing Prompt

Write whether you think Alan and Joe's plan was cheating or was a fair strategy. Make sure you give reasons to support your answer.

_____

_____

_____

_____

_____

_____

_____

_____

_____

Guided Close Reading

Closely reread the beginning of chapter 28. Stop at, ". . . went off to the bathroom to take two aspirin."

Directions: Think about these questions. In the space below, write ideas as you think about the answers. Be ready to share your answers.

❶ Look back at the book. Where does Joe hide?

❷ What details from the text show that Alan's father and mother are not happy with him?

❸ Based on the events in the story, why does Billy wake up the whole neighborhood in the middle of the night?

Making Connections-Worm Recipe

Directions: Billy's father challenges Billy's mother to make some interesting worm dishes for Billy. He suggests poached eels on toast, spaghetti with wormballs, savory worm pie, and even creamed worms on toast. Pick a dish that is mentioned in chapter 21 or 22, and write a recipe for it. Include a list of ingredients you would need and instructions for the dish's preparation.

Recipe

Directions	Ingredients
_____	_____
_____	_____
_____	_____
_____	_____
_____	_____
_____	_____
_____	_____
_____	_____

Name _____ Date _____

Language Learning–Onomatopoeia

Directions: This section of the book has many onomatopoeia words. Look through chapter 27 and chapter 29 to find four onomatopoeia words. Write them on the lines below and draw a picture to illustrate each word.

Language Hints!

- Onomatopoeia are words that imitate the natural sounds of words, such as *buzz* or *oink*.

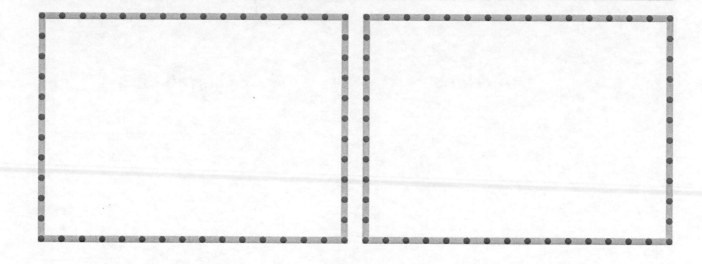

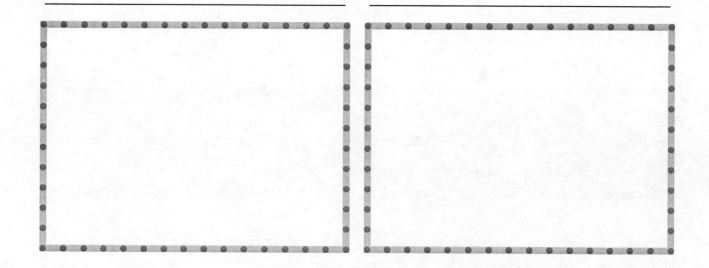

Story Elements-Setting

Directions: Draw a picture of Billy, Tom, and Pete outside of Alan's house in the middle of the night from chapter 27. Make sure to include details such as the house lights in the neighborhood, the worm, and all the characters. Then, write at least three sentences describing the setting.

_____

_____

_____

_____

Story Elements-Plot

Directions: Draw a cartoon of the fight between the four boys in chapter 29. Include speech bubbles for the characters' thoughts and/or what they say. Choose carefully since you can include only six images.

Vocabulary Overview

Key words and phrases from this section are provided below with definitions and sentences about how the words are used in the story. Introduce and discuss these important vocabulary words with students. If you think these words or other words in the story warrant more time devoted to them, there are suggestions in the introduction for other vocabulary activities (page 5).

Word	Definition	Sentence about Text
staggered (ch. 32)	walked or moved unsteadily	A shaken Billy staggers across the room to the sink.
feebly (ch. 32)	in a manner that shows a lack of strength	Billy feebly drew himself a glass of water.
defrauding (ch. 33)	to get money by tricking or cheating someone	Tom wonders if his friends could be arrested for defrauding the mail.
suspiciously (ch. 34)	distrustfully; in a way that shows that you think something might be wrong	Billy glances around the barn suspiciously.
concede (ch. 34)	surrender	On the last day of the bet, Joe tells Billy that he concedes.
cistern (ch. 36)	an underground container that is used for storing water	A crazed Alan suggests putting Billy down in the old cistern.
babble (ch. 37)	the confusing sound of many people speaking at the same time	There is a confused babble of voices in the barn.
cavorting (ch. 40)	jumping or moving around in a lively manner	The boys celebrate, with dog Pete cavorting beside them.
slunk off (ch. 40)	walked off in a way that does not attract attention, usually because you are embarrassed	Finally defeated, Alan and Joe slink off through the bushes.
smoldering (ch. 41)	burning slowly without flames	The boys meet by a smoldering fire on the riverbank.

Name _____ Date _____

Vocabulary Activity

Directions: Practice your vocabulary and writing skills. Write at least four sentences using words from the story. Make sure your sentences show what the words mean.

Words from the Story

staggered	feebly	defrauding	suspiciously	concede
cistern	babble	cavorting	slunk off	smoldering

_____

_____

_____

_____

_____

_____

_____

_____

Directions: Answer this question.

1. Why does Alan try to put Billy in the **cistern**?

_____

_____

Analyzing the Literature

Provided here are discussion questions you can use in small groups, with the whole class, or for written assignments. Each question is written at two levels so that you can choose the right question for each group of students. For each question, a few key points are provided for your reference as you discuss the book with students.

Story Element	Level 1	Level 2	Key Discussion Points
Character	Why do Alan's father and Mr. O'Hara want the boys to talk things over?	In chapter 30 the boys sit down together. Does it seem like they truly work things out?	Alan's father and Mr. O'Hara want the boys to work things out because the four of them have been friends for so long. They don't want the friendship to be destroyed. The boys are still angry and resentful. They discuss the fight and the cheating but don't really resolve anything. Joe says that he is resigned to the fact that Billy will win the bet. But his statements seem a little fishy, and he cuts off Alan when he tries to disagree.
Plot	In this section, what three strategies do Alan and Joe use to try to keep Billy from winning the bet?	How do Alan and Joe's tricks change as the days pass and Billy gets closer to winning the bet?	Alan and Joe send a fake letter to Billy's house, trying to fool Billy into thinking that Dr. McGrath is concerned for his health. The next day they serve Billy a phony worm that is made of beans. Finally, Alan locks Billy in a closet and tries to put him in a cistern. As the end of the 15 days approaches, the boys become more desperate. Their sabotages become better and more elaborate. The final attempt to stop Billy is violent and dangerous. It is clear that this bet has brought out the worst in Joe and Alan.
Setting	What is the setting of chapters 36 and 37?	How does the setting of chapters 36 and 37 contribute to the scary turn the story takes?	Chapters 36 and 37 take place in the deserted horse barn near Billy's house. The barn becomes a scary place because it is isolated, set away from the house and any watchful parents. Alan is able to lock Billy in a tool closet. He also tries to put Billy down an old cistern, which would be extremely dangerous.

Reader Response

Think

The boys make a bet for 50 dollars. If you wanted 50 dollars, what could you do to get the money? Think about ways you could earn money.

Informative/Explanatory Writing Prompt

Write how you could earn 50 dollars. Be sure to include all the steps it would take to get that amount of money.

_____

_____

_____

_____

_____

_____

_____

_____

_____

Guided Close Reading

Closely reread chapter 41, "Epiloguc."

Directions: Think about these questions. In the space below, write ideas as you think about the answers. Be ready to share your answers.

❶ What information from the text shows that Billy wins the bet and buys what he wants?

❷ What evidence tells the reader how Alan is paying for the bet?

❸ Use details from the book to prove that Billy still likes to eat worms.

Name _____ Date _____

Making Connections—
Invertebrates or Vertebrates?

Directions: Almost all animals are classified as one of two groups—invertebrates or vertebrates. Invertebrates are animals without backbones. Vertebrates are animals with backbones. Worms are invertebrates. Cut out the pictures of the animals below and glue them under the correct headings on page 57. Classify each animal as either an invertebrate or a vertebrate.

bee	monkey	rabbit	dolphin
snail	kangaroo	worm	dog
bird	spider	frog	jellyfish

Making Connections–
Invertebrates or Vertebrates? *(cont.)*

Directions: Glue the animals from page 56 under the correct headings below.

Invertebrates	Vertebrates

Language Learning–Punctuation

Directions: Below are several modified sentences from *How to Eat Fried Worms*. Rewrite each sentence using quotation marks correctly.

Language Hints!

- Put quotation marks around the words spoken by the characters.
- A comma usually separates the quotation from the rest of the sentence.

1. We'll be out in the kitchen said Alan's father.

   _____

   _____

2. Did you have stitches? Billy asked Alan.

   _____

   _____

3. I can't get the money till tomorrow he said.

   _____

   _____

4. I've won crowed Billy.

   _____

   _____

Story Elements-Character

Directions: Think about what you know about the characters in the book. In the chart below, describe each character by writing at least three descriptive words or phrases next to his name.

Billy			
Alan			
Tom			
Joe			

Name _____ Date _____

Story Elements-Plot

Directions: Add a scene to this last chapter of the book. Describe the setting, characters, and any dialogue that might take place. Be creative!

_____

_____

_____

_____

_____

_____

_____

_____

_____

_____

_____

_____

Post-Reading Theme Thoughts

Directions: Choose a main character from *How to Eat Fried Worms*. Pretend you are that character. Draw a picture of a happy face or a sad face to show how the character would feel about each statement below. Then use words to explain your picture.

Character I Chose: _____

Statement	How Does the Character Feel? ☺ ☹	Explain Your Answer
Bets are fun to make but hard to keep.		
When kids are worried, they should talk to their parents.		
Friends disagree sometimes.		
Cheating is not fair.		

Culminating Activity:
The Importance of Characters

Directions: Choose one of the following activities.

Write and illustrate your own new adventure of the four boys: Alan, Joe, Billy, and Tom. Base the story on your own experiences with friends, as well as the character backgrounds you know about the four boys. For example, you could write *How to Make Up with Friends* or *Mini-bike Adventures*. To create the book, use copies of the Storybook Sheet on page 63.

Decide which of the four boys is your favorite and draw a life-size figure of him on bulletin board paper. Around the edges of your drawing, write words to describe the character's unique traits. Your words should express why he is your favorite character from the story. Include details from the story in your descriptive words.

Make puppets of at least six characters from the story. Write a short skit and turn it into a puppet show. Make sure the characters interact with each other in ways that are true to the original story.

Create a three-dimensional model of the setting and the characters. You may use supplies like cardboard, construction paper, sticks, grass, clay, craft sticks or anything else you find helpful to create your display.

Storybook Sheet

Directions: Use this page if you choose to write and illustrate your own new adventure for the four boys.

Name _____ Date _____

Comprehension Assessment

Directions: Fill in the bubble for the best response to each question.

Section 1

1. What kind of worms does Billy specify he will **not** eat?

   Ⓐ worms from the butcher shop

   Ⓑ night crawlers

   Ⓒ the big green worms from the tomato plants

   Ⓓ worms from the manure pile

Section 2

2. Why can't Alan sleep?

   Ⓔ He has a nightmare.

   Ⓕ Joe wakes him up.

   Ⓖ His father wakes him up.

   Ⓗ He is worried he will lose the bet.

Section 3

3. How does Billy figure out he is being tricked on the ninth worm?

   Ⓐ He hears Alan and Joe talking about their plan.

   Ⓑ Tom tells him.

   Ⓒ He scrapes cornmeal off the worm and sees glue.

   Ⓓ The worm is two feet long.

Comprehension Assessment *(cont.)*

Section 4

4. In what way does the boys asking Mrs. Forrester to be the referee help Billy?

_____

_____

_____

_____

_____

Section 5

5. Why does the fifteenth worm seem suspicious to Billy?

(E) It tastes like beans.

(F) It is much too long.

(G) It is hidden inside a cake.

(H) It is boiled, not fried.

Response to Literature:
To Trick or Not to Trick?

Directions: Pretend you are Billy. Write a letter to Alan and Joe telling them how you feel about their many attempts to trick you. Did the ways that they try to win the bet affect your friendship?

Dear Alan and Joe,

_____

_____

_____

_____

_____

_____

_____

_____

_____

_____

From,

Billy

Response to Literature: (cont.)

1. What is the meanest trick that Alan and Joe pull on Billy?

_____

_____

_____

_____

2. What do you learn about Billy from Alan and Joe's attempts to trick Billy throughout the book?

_____

_____

_____

_____

3. Choose another character from the book, such as Tom or one of the parents. How do Alan and Joe's attempts to cheat affect that character?

_____

_____

_____

_____

Name _____ Date _____

Response to Literature Rubric

Directions: Use this rubric to evaluate student responses.

Great Job	Good Work	Keep Trying
☐ You answered all three questions completely. You included many details.	☐ You answered all three questions.	☐ You did not answer all three questions.
☐ Your handwriting is very neat. There are no spelling errors.	☐ Your handwriting can be neater. There are some spelling errors.	☐ Your handwriting is not very neat. There are many spelling errors.
☐ Your letter is complete with at least three details.	☐ Your letter is mostly complete with at least two details.	☐ Your letter is not complete.
☐ Creativity is clear in both the letter and the questions.	☐ Creativity is clear in either the letter or the questions.	☐ There is not much creativity in the letter or the questions.

Teacher Comments: _____

_____

_____

_____

The responses provided here are just examples of what students may answer. Many accurate responses are possible for the questions throughout this unit.

Vocabulary Activity—Section 1:
Chapters 1–6 (page 15)

1. The boys want witnesses to make sure that Billy eats all the worms and does not cheat.

Guided Close Reading—Section 1:
Chapters 1–6 (page 18)

1. The boys are arguing over where to dig the first worm. Joe says they can get them anywhere they want. Tom says, "Not from a manure pile," and "That's not fair."

2. Joe says, "There is nothing wrong with manure," and "It comes from cows, just like milk."

3. Tom asks his friends, "Would you eat a worm from a manure pile?"

Language Learning—Section 1:
Chapters 1–6 (page 20)

1. what is
2. would not
3. has not
4. I will
5. can not
6. did not
7. had not
8. they will
9. it will
10. he is

Vocabulary Activity—Section 2:
Chapters 7–13 (page 24)

- Billy eats **steadily,** grimacing, rubbing his nose, spreading on horseradish.

- I can't help thinking of a worm squirming as the fishhook **gores** into him.

- Alan and Joe watch from above, lying on their stomachs in the **hayloft.**

- Billy spins around just in time to catch a glimpse of Tom **pelting** out the door.

- Joe looks at Billy **sullenly** because he is upset about something that Billy said.

1. Billy is constantly thinking of **gaggles** of worms because he is preoccupied with worrying about the bet and whether he can actually eat 15 worms.

Guided Close Reading—Section 2:
Chapters 7–13 (page 27)

1. Joe says, "Come on. We haven't got all day." Alan adds, "Five more minutes. Then I win."

2. Billy hears Alan and Joe whispering, "He's gonna quit," and "I knew he'd never make it when I bet with him."

3. After eating the fifth worm, Billy wipes his gooey hands on Alan's trousers while he grins messily at him.

Making Connections—Section 2:
Chapters 7–13 (pages 28–29)

The Body of an Earthworm

Earthworms have no arms, legs, lungs, or eyes.

Earthworms breathe through their skin. They surface after heavy rains so they do not drown.

Even though earthworms have no eyes, they can sense light.

Earthworms have five hearts.

Each earthworm is both male and female.

Where Earthworms Live

Earthworms live in soil, trees, and under rocks.

Earthworms live where there is food, moisture, oxygen, and a good temperature.

Earthworms can burrow up to six feet (1.83 meters) deep.

Different Kinds of Earthworms

In the Philippines there are blue earthworms.

The night crawler gets its name because it typically surfaces after dark.

There are thousands of different kinds of earthworms.

South African earthworms can grow to be 22 feet (6.71 meters) long.

Language Learning—Section 2:
Chapters 7–13 (page 30)

Students' responses will vary, but may include the following adjectives: slimy, gross, slippery, gooey, yucky, disgusting, greasy, scary, dirty, and stinky.

Story Elements—Section 2:
Chapters 7–13 (page 32)

Events will vary, but they should be in chronological order.

Vocabulary Activity—Section 3:
Chapters 14–19 (page 34)

1. Alan is so worried about the bet, he **gnaws** at his fingernails.

2. Billy dreams he must eat a **mammoth** worm.

3. Tom is unsure of how Billy feels, so he waves **tentatively** at Billy.

4. Outside, the wind blows and Billy hears a **shutter** banging.

5. Billy thinks he needs an **antidote** because he is afraid the worms might be poisonous and he might be sick from eating them.

Guided Close Reading—Section 3:
Chapters 14–19 (page 37)

1. Billy puts mustard on the worm and later swooshes it into ketchup and horseradish sauce.

2. "Alan couldn't get the fifty dollars out of his head." He wonders what his father is "going to say when he told him he'd bet fifty dollars and lost." He gnaws at his thumbnail.

3. Billy laughs at Alan. He says, "You think you can scare me talking like that? Phooey."

Making Connections—Section 3:
Chapters 14–19 (page 38)

1. Billy would need to eat **6** worms each day.

2. Billy would eat **45** worms altogether.

3. Billy would need to eat **5** worms each day.

Language Learning—Section 3:
Chapters 14–19 (page 39)

Students' definition might be along the lines of:

- **jostled**: bumped against someone when in a crowd
- **discernible**: perceptible; able to be seen
- **serene**: calm and peaceful
- **glowered**: looked at in an angry way
- **sheepishly**: in a way that shows embarrassment, especially when you know you have done something foolish

Vocabulary Activity—Section 4:
Chapters 20–29 (page 43)

1. slumped
2. murmur
3. clenched
4. weasel out
5. Joe says that Billy's mother will make a good **referee** because she is usually pretty fair, and because parents almost never cheat kids if it's just something between kids.

Guided Close Reading—Section 4:
Chapters 20–29 (page 46)

1. Joe hides under the bed, peeking out through the fringe of the bedspread.

2. Alan's father drags him back from the window. He yells, "Quiet!" and sits Alan down hard in a chair. Alan's mother throws up her hands and goes off to the bathroom to take two aspirin.

3. Billy wakes up the whole neighborhood because he is mad that Alan and Joe tried to use a baseball game to distract him from eating his daily worm. Billy wants to show the boys that he is not tricked, and that he is still on track to win the bet. He also wants to embarrass them because he feels betrayed by their maneuvers.

Answer Key

Language Learning—Section 4:
Chapters 20–29 (page 48)

Possible onomatopoeia words include: chomp, screech, squawk, chirp, bark, spiffle, whack, thump, thwomp, womp, and donk.

Vocabulary Activity—Section 5:
Chapters 30–41 (page 52)

1. Alan tries to put Billy in the cistern so he will be trapped, will not eat the last worm, and will lose the bet.

Guided Close Reading—Section 5:
Chapters 30–41 (page 55)

1. "Billy landed the mini-bike against a tree . . ."

2. Alan is working: "Where's Alan? At the store?" "He's still got two weeks to go."

3. Billy's lunch is a worm-and-egg on rye. He says, "I don't know. I just can't stop. I don't tell my mother. I even like the taste now." He wonders if he might be hooked on worms.

Making Connections—Section 5:
Chapters 30–41 (pages 56–57)

Invertebrates	Vertebrates
bee	monkey
snail	rabbit
spider	dolphin
worm	frog
jellyfish	kangaroo
	bird
	dog

Language Learning—Section 5:
Chapters 30–41 (page 58)

1. "We'll be out in the kitchen," said Alan's father.

2. "Did you have stitches?" Billy asked Alan.

3. "I can't get the money till tomorrow," he said.

4. "I've won!" crowed Billy.

Story Elements—Section 5:
Chapters 30–41 (page 59)

Answers will vary, but may include:

- **Billy:** competitive, determined, stubborn, humorous, fair, adventurous eater

- **Alan:** tricky, deceitful, worried, regretful

- **Tom:** good friend, helpful, talks big, picky eater

- **Joe:** devious, sly, schemer, sneaky

Comprehension Assessment
(pages 64–65)

1. C. the big green worms from the tomato plants

2. H. He is worried he will lose the bet.

3. C. He scrapes cornmeal off the worm and sees glue.

4. Mrs. Forrester makes the worms taste better by putting them in dishes such as Alsatian Smothered Worm and Whizbang Worm Delight. She also makes Billy feel better about the bet simply by supporting him and therefore erasing his concern that the worms might be poisonous.

5. E. It tastes like beans.